D1526474

QUICK, NOW, ALWAYS

Poems by

Mark Irwin

❦

BOA Editions, Ltd. ❦ Brockport, NY ❦ 1996

LC #: 95–79997
ISBN: 1–880238–30–6 cloth
ISBN: 1–880238–31–4 paper

First Edition
96 97 98 99   7 6 5 4 3 2 1

Publications by BOA Editions, Ltd.—
a not-for-profit corporation under section 501 (c) (3)
of the United States Internal Revenue Code—
are made possible with the assistance of grants from
the Literature Program of the New York State Council on the Arts
and the Literature Program of the National Endowment for the Arts,
the Lannan Foundation,
as well as from the Rochester Area Foundation Community Arts Fund
administered by the Arts & Cultural Council for Greater Rochester,
the County of Monroe, NY,
and from many individual supporters.

Cover Art: Intaglio print, "Excitement on the Way Down"
by Douglas Dibble
Cover Photo: Earl Kage
Cover Design: Daphne Poulin-Stofer
Author Photo: Lisa Utrata
Typesetting: Richard Foerster
Manufacturing: McNaughton & Gunn, Lithographers
BOA Logo: Mirko

BOA Editions, Ltd.
A. Poulin, Jr., President
92 Park Avenue
Brockport, NY 14420

for Reyes García & Ronald Marvell
for Lisa & Heather

For even the nearest moment is far from mankind.

—Rilke
Seventh Duino Elegy

CONTENTS

FOUR

❧❧❧

ONE

Is it not well done that our language has but one word for all kinds of love, from the holiest to the most lustfully fleshly? All ambiguity is therein resolved: love cannot but be physical, at its farthest stretch of holiness; it cannot be impious, in its utterest fleshliness. It is always itself, as the height of shrewd "geniality" as in the depth of passion; it is organic sympathy, the touching sense-embrace of that which is doomed to decay.

—Thomas Mann
The Magic Mountain

AS LONG AS

The heart's vaulting path. The quiet storms of their flesh,
And behind the purple irises, fire, a faster stair, while the vast
Armatures of twilight and dusk made them drunk with it:

The gluey gold light illumined the ostrich ferns, and the fireweed,
Its fuchsia bloom. Their lips, wet, zipped the silence together as
Long as they did not stop, as long as their eyes remained closed,

As long as there was no plan, no thought, no logos, but lust,
Things would remain whole? And they would hold that pose till
    the fire goes
Out, till the light became less and less, till the sheer current

Left their limbs, released, and they could simply open their eyes
And leave and not see one another, but feel that braille primal
    surge
From above. The slow pendulum of stars, their crystal torque in
    the dark.

❦

BUCHAREST, 1981

Damian, thank you for Constantine's
book, which I have opened only
once, but keep reading in my sleep.

I remember walking over to your flat,
after having crossed Athènée Palace
Square, and thinking that I saw

Domnica's face. She could not leave.
The Securitate followed me.
I could not write.

Damian, thank you for Constantine's
book, which I have opened only
once, but keep reading in my sleep.

Afraid, I kept seeing Domnica's
face. Once, outdoors, she poured
water from a silver pitcher
into a glass vase

toward which her blond hair spilled;
now I cannot sleep. Damian
thank you for Constantine's
book, which I opened

once to three slips of paper,
certificates: birth, marriage, death,
enclosed in his application for

passport. Everyone in this poem
is dead, except one girl, pouring light or water,
and myself, reading very late at night.

VISTA

for Ron Kroutel

I can almost recognize this from the hill,
the grey ribbon of highway leading into town, the overpass, its
antique colonnade shouldering the sun, and the way the sky falls
like blue snow through the steel towers
of the Electrical Park

locking everything into place. Home
looks out a picture window
that looks out upon trees
where a few deer stray like words
on a screen. We are so lonely

for this view, lonely to make
words in the small world
inside our homes. And while the children
were singing the squat snowman up, Sal
was dying in his garage. Sal who built

most of these homes. And then Willa screaming
off the deck, "Sal is dead." The words
hang there still, somewhere between
the gas barbecue and pool. And then we all wrote
cards: "Willa, deepest regards for you

in this difficult time." —Words
shy, words that kept slipping off
the page. It's summer now, that's why I say
I can almost recognize all this from the hill. I can still see

Sal. He dug the foundation for most of our
homes. He was the yellow hat and tiny waving hand
sitting high up in the backhoe's brain. I watched him
push rocky chunks of ground. Once his dirt-caked hands
lifted me high with the words "Did you

know I built your Dad's home?" I remember
that, and I remember Willa's scream: blue
electric words that still hang in the air
between the gas barbecue and pool. That was the day
the mailman disappeared into the woods.

❧

ALMOST NEVER

The sun, dimesize and cool, in the 5 o'clock sky.
Always, it seldom moves. And the entire family of shadows,
Each one cast, distinct, breathyblack, against the ochre stone

Wall. Womanshadow, manshadow, and lesser boy and girl
Shadow too. You can tell gender by their shadow
Hair. Trees whisper

Schhh, willows I believe, where the creek trickles
Through the courtyard. Flocked shadows blurry
There; light glyphs where the water pools,

Pools like greed, glassy and full. God how they would love
Endlessly to sup there, till the surface, mirrory,
Shoos them away, but memory

Will come to them, just as it has come to me—.
The castiron skillet on the stove. Dawn. Calyx of jetblue
Flame. Hiss of steam. Coffee smell, its wet blossom

Sagging down. Or my wife— tan, ripe, —bending in the June
Garden and incandescent air. Weeds gently tugging at her
Hands. Clouds—, cumulus—, sheer, jellied and full,

Sweating light out over the body's work, its sweet will; over The
starling's limegreen eye, his head a purple iridescent
Hue. Rain, small, collecting on our sweaty skin;

Mushrooms, new, sleek and inky wet, except the breathing
Gills. A cardinal's *twuuu*. The trout, cleaned, their rose
And lavender sides, speckled, quaking till—-. These things, more

Now, yet ephemeral, still. I can almost feel my blood
Warming in the sun. How slowly memories return
Unsummoned. One day, somewhere near, I saw

Two kids running, their blond arms paddling
Through the wheat's seaswell. But when I looked again,
Their sugary breaths rose like steam over a plowed field.

How slow-cold eternity. You see, seasons are our days.
Now late autumn's evening comes. Don't worry,
I want to whisper through the yellow

Wind. Go to sleep. Night will come. But their shadows
Grow slant and longer, as though the sun
Had moved. You see, just as on earth, it scares them to be free.

☙❧

THE JUVESCENCE OF AUTUMN

At dusk the ambulance came
pulling all the way up onto the lawn
like a red speedboat drifting

* * *

ashore. She was old.
She had fallen and broken her pelvis
while picking apples. She had

* * *

pruned that tree so many times
it appeared as a dark
hood. About it her white

* * *

head moved. The attendants, unloading
the gurney, argued about whose turn
it was to buy the pizza. I had been

* * *

sitting outside, reading beneath the yellow
leaves. I heard the thin
cry. She said to call, but that she

* * *

was OK, except for the pain. Then there was
nothing to say. We stared at the apples
still nested in their thick green hive. She talked

* * *

of a daughter, her grandchildren, her
dead husband, Karl. Still she stared
at the tree, talking as if the fruit

* * *

restored memory. That was the day a *streaker*
ran all the way down Bellflower Lane.
The sudden white breasts, — the pale shadow

* * *

between legs. Now I finally remember
what I wanted to say. —The silver thread
of the siren the ambulance followed

* * *

away. And that tree, the swollen
green crown, on which the apples were cities
opening far out onto an invisible blue world.

❧

ARCHBISHOP OF CANTERBURY RAMSEY
AND THE BISHOP OF SOUTHWICK

Photograph by Robert Mapplethorpe (1975)

That we could not be careless without wilderness
seems a condition. The archbishop's robe looks more scarlet
than crimson. He sits on the burnished oak bench
next to the big-leaved tree, and leans slightly back
holding a martini. They talk casually

but with concern. Twilight encroaches. The archbishop's
shoes have large square silver buckles. The lightfall,
gold on the lawn, seems to fasten the black
leather to them. At times in his studio
the young photographer would say, "I think
I am dying." I think of the photograph
of the girl, freckled, on the church steps holding her hem

down. The portraits of black oiled men seem
invulnerable as bronzes, but their lips usually hidden
flower. And the flowers, the calla lilies, beautifully
sterile, remind one more of marble
than of flowers. There are no bees on the flowers.

No flowers in this photo. The bishop's purple
jacket at times appears violet. It rises above the green
and embraces the evening. The gold silk tie
like a flame suspends him. Why are there
no birds visible in the garden? The bishop speaks
with concern, but confidence. After all,
this is not wilderness, but a garden. That knowledge deports us

is certain, but from a wilderness of desire
came all gardens. The archbishop's crimson robe
slightly reclines with the body. The white shock of hair
floats on the head that centers the photo. It speaks
of silence, compassion, and listening. There is something wildly

operatic about the setting. "Free to choose everything," he
considers, "would one be devoured by his choices?
Could there be hope after such freedom?" The pimento
garnishes the olive, the martini
our actions. Would a garden be spontaneous
through the bees' random equation?
The burnished oak bench

sinks in the evening. The bishop's purpling vestment
recedes from the viewer. The petals
of a magnolia open. A man
gives himself to another. Scarlet
the archbishop's robe approaches. That we are an iridescent

vanishing chaos, and that art is a farther city
is both the failed wondrance
and beauty of evening. Beauty's truth
is fast; truth a
stasis. That by breaking the form of the body
we might allow the work to depart. The archbishop
and bishop speak casually, but finally

no matter what, they discuss what
the artist is thinking. Flowers, people, art.
Art flowers with people. How do we constellate desire
when what we exalt becomes
guttered? The work of art is beyond. We perish

to complete it. The light is unusually gold
this evening. A man lifts
another up from sleep. I did not know
that among the dead one could found a new
city. The bishop and archbishop speak casually. The lunacy
of their hands is a quiet language. There are no birds
in the garden. Into the closing dusk will the violet or scarlet fade
    sooner?

❦

J.F.K.'s 45 BIRTHDAY:
MADISON SQUARE GARDEN

The great cake, four tiers high, stood
like Lincoln's hat, tall as a century,
and was carried out by two New York chefs
on an army stretcher, as the lights were dimmed
and the candles lit, and Marilyn arrived
so very late, late in the 20th

century. She tiptoed out onto the stage
in a white mink stole, during Civil Rights,
during the Cold War, after DiMaggio, and after Miller,
and began in a blousy almost whispering voice
to sing "Happy Birthday," emancipating for all who watched,
desire, what love will never waste in tired history.

~ℰ~

RUMORS OF CIVILIZATION AND HISTORY

That morning, July 5th, he found among grass
Shredded bits of a Chinese newspaper, its disembodied
Characters, and the frayed husk of a sky rocket
Still attached to its splintered raspberry stem.
Last night's celebration lingers in the mind:

Showers of diamonds, rubies, shattered emeralds,
The slowly paced colors of a roman candle,
Their pause and held breath of thunder
Remembered now like a wealthy hangover.
Independence, the subconscious of a nation.

Next door, a boy, finger wet with spit,
Traces circles on the window, stares out
At the oncoming storm. In three hours
The rain makes the circles reappear.
Dissolution and the return to form.

Distant in their nearness, church bells ride the air
Among the clouds of afternoon. Peal after
Hollow peal, they reconstruct a brief history,
The music of suffering and forgiveness.
Towards evening he thinks about time,

The way the present jars our lives,
How it contains both past and future.
The packed suitcase of a man now dead
Travels on forever in our minds
That wear his clothes like gestures
Failed. Entrances without invitation.

Finally, all seems distilled to the personal
History of the future. A man sits looking
At the vacant pages of a scrapbook, white spaces
Transposed to fog, tablets of stone, the grass
And sunlight. What makes him sad, is that there
In the shade, a bird has already begun its singing.

WHITE

My father is dead, yet
how beautiful the snow.
For weeks now I've
done nothing, no thing

at all. But today
I stare out my window
and watch the snow
fall. Heavily, more heavily

still, the thick white flakes
soon mask the air, and slowly
I begin the long walk through
fields. There a white church

stands, but I do not
go in, no, I just stare
slowly stare until slowly
that church disappears.

❦

TWO

Le Paradis n'est pas artificiel
                        but is jagged . . .

—Ezra Pound

AIRPORT

Sun extends the sky— and the jets,
Sleek aluminum pods,
Nose up against
The glass. Corridors

Dissolve. Passengers
Shuffle and queue
Suddenly enclosed
In a brief church of

Farewells. Light floods
Concrete and cloud. Wings
Glint beneath sun. Planes
Taxi, turn, glide; toys

Moved by an invisible hand.
Turbines whir, subside; a
High-pitched suck and whine.
Where is the outside of our

Lives? Acres of cement disclose
The horizoned trees, wavy
And dumb through the fueled
Heat.—A readying

Jet. Light, tinseled, leaks
Along its side—turning,
A tube of windows,
Faces, illumined, dissolves.

❧

BUFFALO NICKEL

Listen, can you hear the faint drone of sirens
moving through a river of cars? They are a violence
tattooed on cities, and we lean like plants
from the stems of our bodies, lean as toward

* * *

the drone of the sea. We need a new coin
with a jet on one side and on the other,
God. What would he look like?—Jambalaya
of noise. —A city's recrudescence

* * *

of glare. *Engine Rock*, aboriginal its orangish-
red glow. Reptilian, —all escarpment and scale.
Ochre are its bones, bleached pink and lavender its ashy

* * *

halo. The Nebraskan sun gold on their horns,
at dusk their wooly hair like smoke. As a boy in New York
I touched one, held the clear, bright language of myth

* * *

on a nickel. Wilderness is where
we never wander. And where, and where

* * *

and where. Dusk, the ghostly pastels of a few TV's
shimmer in Taos Pueblo. Where the creek divides
the kivas, a few beer cans tinsel the ground. —Trash

* * *

offerings up to some divinity? What did you
discover today? In La Junta, a man was trampled
by his own horses. The limits of the land,

* * *

the limits of the body. Buffalo, brown-matted fungus of God.
Home is not here, but there, not now, but then.

❧

GORGE

By the creek's quartz light
The trout lie quaking
With life. The slow bellows
Of their scarlet gills fade,
Like the tips of the oak leaves,
And only half-breathe.

Acorns tick down this gorge
Over five million years
Old. Intaglio fins and bones
Swim on broken pieces of shale
And resemble the larger
Skeletal remains of pines.

The river with its bouldery
Spine wallows in a stone-
Ripened and clay-shadow
Light. The frying pan hisses
And pops. By my feet
A palette of gutted remains,

Above, the crests of wooden trees
Flame, blood-red, ochre, tangerine,
Then, one by one, succumb
To a triangular wall of shade.
The chill air carries the frost-
Rich scent of nut and clove.

Low in the west, Venus
Rises, a white-hot drop
Of lead. Already drenched
With night, I eat the sweet
Flesh, then carefully lay
The bones back into the fire.

&&&

ORPHEUS

Before the end, before the lovers spoke only in numbers,
before the photographs replaced memory, before vanity became a
    form
of passion and chic men and women stood idly before the great
airports of death, Orpheus

departed, the sheer ambulance of his calm
appalling. And as he guided her toward that light
he sang her whole again, marveling as if for the first time
at hair, ankles, hips, thighs, till the hot fleshy poem
became body, till the lilting rhythm

became her breath, the enjambed lines her reaching
arms, the lyric song an echo
saying, "Look at me, look at the pleasurewash
of creation. Feel the marble now
fleshwarm with salt. —Take

me." He turned once forever. He turned once for every
living thing, and the green waves of the dead became trees
lifted from their graves, listening. He turned
beating the immense immeasurable wings of his song
against the sky of what he knew, of what he knew he had created

from death, of what he had learned from stones, touchdumb
but like her still shivering. He turned
once and turned back willing to be dismembered
so that the fragmented and mounting song
could rise a thousand times more beautiful against nothing.

❧

QUICK, NOW, ALWAYS

We would like to linger here even longer,
especially when the sun lays gold
over lawns, some so white-fenced, idyllic, and sexy
they obsess us with what? —Ourselves? —That recurring
wilderness within? All night the rain
gently sucking leaves till morning. And here
are the flowers that put out our eyes. We should throw
our bodies onto the earth, just as we throw

them onto each other. Reyes and I walked long,
talking of love in a place with no people. We could feel
its absence burning within. First at twilight
in the cow boneyard. Then next morning
beside the birthing pen. The way the heifer licked
the wet calf up, then mooed

life into its bones. This, when nature is
only itself, when love is
sheer will. But still, the mother's eyes bulging
toward the birth, and the mooing that goes down
into the glistening body, down into the soft hooves,
and down into the earth. This mooing
that goes on and on and will not stop, up to
the final sucking ass and carcass of death. This,

what we would, but lack. We choose instead
such sheer reprehensible and pansexual
delights, vogueing us beyond our shirted longing,
incomprehensible despite. Quiet fools we move
and are moved by movings until staring
through the glass eyes of pleasure, we feel its palace

collapse. Oh how we long to feel that muscled
abandon for which there is no height,
an expanse whose taste is
salt, and whose hearing is all underwater,
all struggle, all breathing, one ocean, one
night. Everywhere now new leaves are ungluing, their green
   encased
with light. What we give changes us into something more
airy, something to last.

❧

MOTION

Most of it he remembers as a boy.
A motion finally slowed enough to
See. A motion like a sketch whose
Final joining line inquisitively
Seemed to stray. Is it because
I wonder, that I cannot know?

Saturday mornings, the bank he stood
In front of. His fingers fast and working
Silkyblack with news. The swish of
Papers sold. He held them by his chest,
Headlines facing out. The day's events
He could become? As a boy becomes

A man? He liked a girl. They sweated
In a car. She had a child. There was
A war. He volunteered to kill. He
Watched straw huts burn, the way
Orange rhymes with red, and youth
Tends to be misled? Finally, home.

Everyone had changed. His mother's face
Suddenly fleshed with age. His wife,
Daughter, gone, yet saddened he could
No longer feel, but remembered how once
Among the dead, he gazed up at stars.
Is it desire that nothing cannot be?

✿✿✿

TOMATO SOUP

The simplicity of unadorned taste:
tomatoes, flour, salt. Unceremonious
and so unlike an English stew.

No hidden bones, chunks of meat.
No skeletons in our closet.
Can of soup, can of water.

You eat it after doing simple things:
skating, skiing, or just taking a walk
down a street of look-alike homes.

No iron kettle to hide ingredients.
A stainless steel pot on an electric range
works best. Do not add salt or pepper.

The simplicity of unadorned taste.
We love it the way the Italians
love tomato sauce with basil:

as a stronghold of culture,
a stubborn remembrance of revolution,
of green vines tied to stakes
and the pendulous warm red fruit.

❧

WARHOL

for Peter Schjeldahl

I watched the working class work and it bored me
to beauty. Something I found in lightbulbs,
sometimes in shoes. Think of it,

a little light shining on someone's empty
shoes, such a small opera, and so ordinary,
but it was the car wrecks

that really saved me. Not that beauty was the beginning
of something scary, but that the scary was beginning
to seem really pretty. Violence

is just so handy, and sometimes love gets
bored to terror. Anyway, so I take
a chair, smear it with lavender,

but it's an electric one. The chair, I mean,
then something begins to happen, a pasteled
violence we can live with, a lavender

disaster. Then the *Maos* and *Marilyns* become
kind of car wrecks, too, but ones
with civilization and culture. Bigger, too!

Portraits so splashy and sugary you could eat them.
Rapture behind which a country's steely
menace grins. I mean

at best we are always watching ourselves
watch. Largely-happy-people
smile, pasted up on so many walls.

I am the world's voyeur, so wallflower
and wooden as to make things sizzle. I love
by remaining indifferent. This is my business, my leisure.

❦

WOOLWORTH'S

for Gerald Stern

Everything stands wondrously multicolored
and at attention in the always Christmas air.
What scent lingers unrecognizably
between that of popcorn, grilled cheese sandwiches,

malted milkballs, and parakeets? Maybe you came here
in winter to buy your daughter a hamster
and were detained by the bin

of *Multicolored Thongs*, four pair
for a dollar. Maybe you came here to buy
some envelopes, the light blue *par avion* ones

with airplanes, but caught yourself, lost,
daydreaming, saying *it's too late* over the glassy
diorama of cakes and pies. Maybe you came here

to buy a lampshade, the fake crimped
kind, and suddenly you remember
your grandmother, dead

twenty years, floating through the old
house like a curtain. Maybe you're retired,
on Social Security, and came here for the *Roast*

Turkey Dinner, or the *Liver and Onions*,
or just to stare into a black circle
of coffee and to get warm. Or maybe

the big church down the street is closed
now during the day, and you're homeless and poor,
or you're rich, or it doesn't matter what you are

with a little loose change jangling in your pocket,
begging to be spent, because you wandered in
and somewhere between the bin of animal crackers

and the little zoo in the back of the store
you lost something, and because you came here
not to forget, but to remember to live.

FOR JACKSON POLLOCK

In April our new black-finned 1957 Ford Fairlane 500
was headed north on Rt. 23
towards Big Stone Gap when a semi-tractor trailer
jackknifed in a thundershower turned hail
and scattered Muriel cigars
all over a green Virginia hillside.
The driver, dazed, was ambulanced away
while my father and dozens of other men
combed that hillside
gathering up the blunts, the panatelas, and the coronas
they lit with so many small fires in the twilight.

And as the sky cleared and the rhododendrons flared gold
as the sun drifting somewhere over Kentucky,
those men continued to discuss
over and over
how the big rig had so benignly split apart,
multiplying the sleek back-haired Gypsie
with the red scarf, red beads, and red lips
all over that green hillside
and how the driver had escaped without so much
as a hangover or a nosebleed.

SPRING

The Navaho boy comes on his bicycle and brings me
food, and I know that it is spring
for the snow lies receding
on Wilson Mesa
where all day I have tended sheep.

He smiles and we
do not speak, though cheese, bread,
and fruit are ample thanks for what I do,
and would keep on doing now, regardless.
And yet I depend on him, and he
depends on me. I gaze

over the San Juan
range. Time
is space: the glacial field that in years
inches moves. Today

a mare foaled
and I lost a ewe.
Coyotes cleaned the bones. Ants
ride along the river of the spine.

The pollen, illumined, is a yellowy-green,
and the trees have taught me
the patience
of being still. Is it

the necessity of vanishing
that brings us home?

The small moon on my thumbnail
for months
drifts over the edge.

At these altitudes, how close
the distance between stone and cloud.

❧

THE FRAY

Sometimes I feel myself tearing
away, forgetting my history and language:
too many stamps with presidents all strangers,
my talk a blur of jargon.

As a child I remember looking down
as if from some great height:
the green houses and red hotels
on a board whose name was like dollars.
How fond I was of rules and colors,
tossing dice and drawing cards of chance.

Now I stand among split-level houses,
the lost hero of a film
dreaming through each of the picture windows
and hollow lives that stray within.

I think of John Kennedy and young America,
Lincoln convertibles and the ghost-light of pennies.
I feel myself moving faster
toward some future's photographed sadness,
saying, we had wild Indians, a California.

❧

THREE

Man becomes, as it were, the sex organs of the machine world, as the bee of the plant world, enabling it to fecundate and to evolve ever new forms.

—Marshall McLuhan
"The Gadget Lover: Narcissus as Narcosis"

TURBO-DESCARTES

1.

I think I am afraid that certainty
is a kind of machine. Duchamp's
nude descends the stairs
where the mechanical rises to abolish

the organic and grown? What does
nature mean now? I know
nothing but the long slow polaroid
we are. To wait is dull; the past

closed, though silksceens of Marilyn and Mao
go on repeating themselves. Do
we resemble one another more
after years in love? Become replicas of
what we build? Lavenderishly

the smog-beaten-sun sets
now, and Hiroshima
never ends—

that painting accomplished
within a second. Now, *now, now* and never
then. Me, *me, me* and never
you. I say

I love you, but somewhere
in between the repetition of vowels
a predictable, self-same music
begins, like those choruses in parts as kids
we sang. If only we could sing

again. Not the turbine's
high-pitched suck
and whine. Not the transformer's
hum. *Let us bow our heads*

the Reverend Moon
said as the rows of snowy brides, 2074
to be exact, all wearing *Simplicity*
Pattern # 8392,
streamed alongside their shadowy grooms
into Madison Square Garden to be

2.

made. When I was a boy
my father did once lift me high
to three large buttons
one *red*   one *black*   one *green*
and gestured with my small hand
toward the would-be-hellish drone.
And I did push the *green*. Like the teething

sounds of the dead, the barely turning steel platens
squeal, as the 1/2 ton Powell River
Canadian paper rolls feed (ink inductors on)
toward the light sensitive aluminum negs
bathed in a greasy stain
that will vomit the world. Oh

I wish you could see
the paper kited high, bridging 12 ft., a blurred Niagara
of grey, as the King Press hummed
with the news which is ink which is
blood. Folded, four pages
per sheet, spit out, conveyered and stacked
until out on the streets

the blind, crippled and poor
would hawk them: **HANOI FALLS, JFK
DEAD, ASTRONAUTS WALK MOON—**
Our passions machined
that the carrier would find,
hands fast and silkyblack with news, bleeding
onto the soap and wash basin

                    3.

to be printed again? New York invents many
lost stories: the homeless one
who had wrapped himself entirely
with newspapers, only his head
like a vulgar eye

exposed as he lay over the sidewalk's
hot air draft, a sort of human kite,
advertising the news, rattling the wind
with words before the spray-painted
wall that read: Graffiti

is God. And for one long moment
it seemed true, in the end
the haphazard

                    4.

word. In the arena of what
is, Joseph the demolitions expert.
We meet at an elegant cocktail
party, and while sipping scotch,
listening to Bach, he tells me
no more *the crane and ball*

but, after the asbestos has been
removed, five strategically placed
charges will bring a fifteen story
building down. He and his wife,
Christine, were soon to be leaving
on a three month cruise. Often I hear a music

in the keening sounds of steel,
and at times its lament rings
from the great bridges we traverse
to the little coins we spend. Spontaneity

5.

is a form of conviction in a conventional
world. *Let's go shopping*, he says. The logo
is easier to buy, than to read.
What you do not understand, tattoo, sell.
I love your lipstick, makeup, your mascaraed
eyes. I love not you, but the possibilities
you incur. Money is a kind of magic

lie. If you don't spend me now, I might
die. He bought an old Methodist church
by the river for a song, gutted and
remodeled it into three condos. Oh
god was good, but god got lost
in his goodness. *I yam what I yam*, Popeye

6.

says. Outside, the entrance,
tuliped and rhododendroned
in spring. Outside among the neon-orange
and red azaleas, where the forsythia's
wicks of yellow phosphor burn. Outside among bees
and the viburnum's rush

of pollen. Outside in the garden,
facing away from the front entrance,
pedestaled in bronze, Rodin's
The Thinker sits,
part of *The Cleveland Museum of Art*
where in the early nineteen seventies
someone at night did place
one stick of lit

dynamite beneath that pedestal.
And the space for a moment did open
above it in an hierophany
of great sacred and social order. And I think
that new wilderness of bronze

was more beautiful
where the torn flanges of green metal
flared upwards like sepals,
and for a long moment that April, the scent
of explosives did linger among flowers
beneath the unscathed head

7.

and torso. The nose
is the last part of the body
to age, yet for most, the first
thing we see. A face enlarged 10X
is projected onto the wall, chiaroscuro

where bone would be carved, then
grafted to the chin. St. Augustine said:
Order is that, which if we keep
it in our lives, leads us to God.
Last night I saw an empty car
idling on the street, and I wanted
to get in. Theory is

8.

a luckless thing. That we are
an accident, all that occurs with the luck and spontaneity
of history's moment, a canvas
whose volcanic city is
distance destroyed. Perfection is finally

9.

a wreckless car. Traveling west
in the still sunny year as my century
darkened to a close, I did stop at Belt Salvage
Inc., just outside of Cortez, where

above the scrapped metal of oil drums,
old Fords, and crippled washers and dryers, I could see
Black Mesa, Lone Cone, and the snowy La Platas
pause for a moment in their descent
to the New Mexican desert.

Here on large wooden pallets
were stacked foot squared cubes of aluminum cans:
candy apple red, lime green, tawdry gold and silver spackle
where drunken bees prowled the pop-top

anthers bright and sticky with
smells of cola and beer. And I remembered
the slow blue, green, and yellow spinning globes
of my childhood. And Christmas was not

10.

far away. Yes far away I did drive at Christmas
from the people and cities I love. And at a
bar in Dolores I met a lady, a very tanked lady,
who introduced herself as Miss E. X.

Love. How delicious the lies we told! The stories more
liberatingly fun. But on New Year's
she lost her subletted trailer. Laughing on our backs
in the Arizona desert, we kissed and parted, after taking
    polaroids

                    11.

of stars. Ours is a sad brief history,
the latter part of the 20th
century: That we are an accident, I sing this upwards
into the minimal. Once outside
what is there to

remember? How beautifully my friend did camouflage
The Statue of Liberty. And though I'm talking
about paint, I do recall the original,
as a child, climbing
up the 142 stairs with my father,

we did peer out from the gilded head
onto the land millioned with possibility. Dream if you will
of a green unrobed beauty, offering up her breasts
from New York Harbor. She rides on a concrete star

blossoming. Against the skyline she stencils
our desires. But I am older
now, and very tired, and want
to make *The Statue*

                    12.

of Nothing Special. I think I am
afraid. This morning my daughter handed
me a note. It said: "You are not my father,
there are no more fathers." Memory
is bankrupt in the 20th century, and forever

13.

is no longer a very long
time. In the back room
of the Hiroshima Peace Museum,
next to the Fuji 3970 Xerox
machine, sits a 4 ft. bronze Buddha
whose face and chest are melted away. I photo-

graphed this with my Kodak
camera. Enlarged 25X,
matted and framed, I placed it on the wall,
behind the black phone on the table
because of the remarkable

14.

resemblance. On a biggish page
I am drawing light bulbs
alongside skulls. I want to blur that distinction
between the frivolous
and the dead. Once, laughing like kids
in a pitch black house, we watched *Gone with the Wind*
on a two inch

black and white TV. How small
we made the world, making love while sirens
and turbines did whir. The last time,
smiling, after we had finished,
your nose

15.

began to bleed. I went to the International Airport,
and after browsing gate after gate
of exotic planes, I chose the blue and white
Pan Am flight 001

around the world. And after all the passengers boarded
and were settled with expectation
and barcoded dreams, the pilot, taxiing,
of homesickness died, and the entire plane
broke into tears. Quietly we gathered
our luggage, and our ruinous desires to make things

16.

new. For six years I looked for my
wife. And after the proceedings began,
the prosecuting attorney asked,
"Did you ever love this man?" She answered,

"I don't even know who he is!"
And the entire courtroom
broke into laughter. And then an inspired silence
occurred, and a beautiful

17.

namelessness prevailed. RAM, floppy disc,
barcode, computer printout.
We have all the information, but at times
don't know how to use it? Has memory become
too perfect? I love the fuzzy

old black and white clip
of Marilyn, all blond and breathy, singing
"Happy Birthday Mr. President." Half-closed eyes
and parted lips, blowing a lullaby
to milky youth. A cameo,

18.

the moon we would use
up? A frontier that moved with each
blousy breath? Is that where it starts?
Or with the Fritz Lang silent, *Frau im Mond*,

1930, after the stock market's
crash. That was the first rocket
countdown launch: 6, 5, 4, 3, 2, 1—
And somewhere Gershwin's rhapsodies,

a last elegant toast? There is
a god I want
sometimes to pray to.
It is the god

19.

of slowness. As a boy
I listened on my transistor radio
to the voice of Houston
through the static
of 230,000 miles. Christmas

in space. They
crossed the Celestial Divide
after having looped
the moon ten times. It
all seemed so strange

20.

and beautiful. To find that wilderness
again in people. Unable
to abide and stay, are we
that lie? I want honest

21.

eyes. I am reading
I have been reading for days
a book entitled *A Brief History
of Desire*. I read the silver words
quickly, but the pages are

22.

lead. Sometimes when I
speak, I feel the edges
of my words. Once I said
"Let's go away,"
and my mouth began
to bleed. If only we could touch

23.

the ocean. In my daughter's room
hangs *The Birth of Venus*.
I love the way Botticelli drew
the toes of the Zephyred

24.

couple.

NOTES

1. (Section 1) Rev. Sun Myung Moon, of the Unification Church, married 2,074 couples at Madison Square Garden in January of 1983.

2. (Section 7) The St. Augustine quote appears in *The Confessions*.

3. (Section 17) Marilyn Monroe (in a surprise celebration) sang "Happy Birthday" to J.F.K. at Madison Square Garden, 1962. It was his 45th birthday.

4. (Section 18) *Frau im Mond* (Woman in Moon) is a silent film by Fritz Lang.

5. (Section 19) Apollo 8, crewed by Borman, Lovell, and Anders, was launched on the morning of December 21, 1968. On Christmas Eve., during their lunar orbit, Anders read the first lines from the Book of Genesis. The event was broadcast over radio and TV.

❦

FOUR

Man makes himself, and he only makes himself completely in proportion as he desacralizes himself and the world. The sacred is the prime obstacle to his freedom. He will become himself only when he is totally demysticized. He will not be truly free until he has killed the last god.

—Mircea Eliade
The Sacred and the Profane

ON LANGUAGE

By a green pond he sits
and watches two swans move
like slow patches of ice
as the pewtery sun
gives way to a hesitant
rain. The page

he reads is
O.K., but its taste
does not spread into his mind
as do the vodka,
cigarette, and scarlet crests
of oaks

until he touches it
to the hot red
ash and sees
how flames doused
by the drying rain
give what slow gold
that poem cannot become,

and more, a tiny blue
crown for nothing's
feckless king,
the drunken soul
through alcohol
lit up posthumously
like a word.

And finally, he wants
no more than in a moment
to forever stall
and mix these contents,
and to drink the wet gold
and violet pulp.

6 AUGUST 1945

I.

Gold priests
drowse with
the sweet

taste of—-.
What is
that lowing

in the skies,
and what city
by sea shore

is emptied?

II.

Leaning a-
gainst Shinjo
Bridge, a

man dead
sitting on
a bicycle.

III.

And the bees
leaned deep-
ly into the

flower, building
their pollen,
a quick

blossom, Hiroshima
in the downwind-
fall of a name.

＊＊＊

GRAND CANYON

Red rock
Sheered by the sun's
Drizzling rays; a steeped haze drops, descends
3 / 4's of a mile
Into the smoky blue
Shade. Down

We move
Through a thousand runneled buttes,
Eroded Byzantiums
Of red-ignited
Sandstone and shale. Pinnacles and minarets
Flame; towers, arches, domes
Dissolve into shadowy plateaus. To the east,

Bruise-blue,
Vishnu's Temple and Wotan's Throne
Support the sky. Above, the putty-white colonnades
—Osiris, Isis— shine.

The canyon walls balloon
With light. Clouds,

Cumulus, drag
Brief lakes of shade.
Purples avalanche grey
Into the inner
Gorge. Down,

Leveling out now
Onto the Tonto Plain,
Its dead sea floor a grey
Reptile head. Cremation
Creek's a pulp of
Dust; heat

Floods up. No
Sound. The last
Sunclad rocks, a skink
Freezes on stone. The sky

Indigo drowsed gold, a jet's
Contrail, the first
Narcotic stars. A cocooned stillness
Tugs us on. Listening
Like children in the storydusk,
We descend toward the river's
Green tongue.

※

HISTORY'S PAUSE

The way maps gradually evolve
toward a kind of truth: Those few cumulus clouds
on a hot Sangre de Cristo afternoon
boiling together to form small continents of

* * *

rain. Rivers divide. Somewhere a child
pulls the threads from an orange. Yellow frontiers
become green territories become organized

* * *

states. In the pupal stage
the larva completely
dissolves. Have you noticed how
in cities the horizon

* * *

disappears? The will of one man
to build a ranch.—From continent's edge,
to horse corral, to his son's
crib. What we cannot enclose

* * *

will not die. New Mexico,
an inextinguishable yellow light
rises up out of

* * *

the land. *Taos, Truth or Consequences, Alamogordo,*
White Sands. Cowboys &

* * *

Indians. Explosion, Sunset.
   Explosion,

* * *

Sunset. Jefferson said: My father was a warrior
so that his son could become a farmer
so that his son could become a

* * *

poet. Hope lay west. From some stationary,
or dead observer, events would appear
to speed up toward

* * *

the horizon. The Golden
Arches of *McDonalds*. *Shell*
gasoline. Yellow

* * *

without. Yellow
within. One million videos
and films, small rivers within culture
leading to an unknown

* * *

where. The contemporary mind
resembles a transistor radio
at night. The roving dial,
the signal that will

* * *

not hold. The cool pastels of a TV
splash across the walls
of the world's

* * *

cartoon. A child rubs his hand
over this late at night. Free we ran

* * *

over the wide open
earth. And love, poor love
atlased beyond our hearts.

THE FACE

Wild and naive,

      always just beyond because of the eyes
      their mystery water rivering out

      time. On the slow field of a cheek
      I have watched blond windlight bend

In a pasturing
curve, the smile's gradual
flood saying come quickly, come quickly

      lest the entire ocean of its
      salt you

Crave change, always, naked and already with-
drawing what you can-
not have.

WE

are out-of-focus and we are
flesh. Some call this panting
love. So much is about
breath. Small at night. Large
in our wakefulness, largest
when the body mates, when the moment
rides on its own rising. Only then
are we safe. —From
ourselves. —Our fears, our hates. Blood.
A little dust and a little water.
Sun and the moist seed
shivers and climbs. Call this blind,
call this a movement toward light.

❧❧❧

WE

have been dead for a long time now
and we have mined all we could from the body,
its fleshy ideal of marble. This city is both
sepulcher and hive, these buildings the future's
gutted memory. But can we really call
this polished *oubliette* history?—When we move like smoke

backwards into the fire. Unmortal we seem
a slow mirror. Some said we must reinvent love,
so we went to speak to the lovers, but the lovers
spoke only in numbers. Beside their forested bedrooms
great dunes of tailings piled high. So much
we wished they were pollen, so much

we dream when we lie! But the soul
in some of us still lingers, a funereal youthfulness
tattooed on bodies. Bodies, bodies, bodies.
With so much desire, what use for
memory? Fire is the chaos
of memory, and history

a slow leaden mirror. Once I loved you
all the way towards a marble city. So
beautiful it was no one
could live there. This, we now call
memory, a magical white glue

still required on statues. Statues
of ourselves we have become, leaning over the night
with a joy which is full. History nor memory nor love
will now help us, so dead we require a park to be full.

TOCK

You play this game slowly before falling asleep.
Each tries to make the softest, barely audible sound,
And it is about all you could never say.

Next to a person you love, *face up to face,*
Start audibly at first, the *sound's* made with your tongue.
You play this game slowly before falling asleep.

The room is swallowed in darkness, but what lies beneath?
Quietly above, the vault of stars moves round,
And it is about all you could never say.

You held her, said you loved her, but she walked away;
Outside stones lie buried deep beneath snow.
You play this game slowly before falling asleep.

Whatever does not occur is yours, forever, to keep.
The stars are no one's mirror. Say *window,* say *home.*
And it is about all you could never say.

Listen long enough and what was color becomes sound.
Against the enormous dark, her small face remains blond.
You play this game slowly before falling asleep,
And it is about all you could never say.

❦

DOMESTIC

December, and it would be a Saturday, some milk
out for the cat, as the long grey evening expires with snow.
He would read, and she would color,
her face pressed right up
against the window of the paper. What does she
see?—Her little heart one joy as the crayon-thick sun
pours yellow out onto the green trees
and large white box, beneath whose triangular hat
they will argue, love, dream, fight, and grow
up in. House. The very word's
a breathing out of so much
breathing in, —a book, a brain,
a wild brilliance of light trying to comprehend the dark air.

❦

ROBERT MAPPLETHORPE'S PHOTOGRAPH
OF APOLLO (1988)

What's missing is the body, its nakedness wrapped
in marble. What's missing is the hair, the floating hair
that falls in chalky tendrils. Only the face, huge
and larval-white, peers into the darkness.
Still, this is perfect youthful manhood, iridescent
against chaos. The eyes, wild and vacant, look
but see nothing. What slaking difference?—
They have known ecstasy, that patina
marble carries everywhere. A suddenness
unwarranted, beautiful. The lips, moistened, part
more to breathe than speak. Such desire,
a poetry. The silk of the moment before him,
the rest becomes salt, memory, history.
There is order here, but passion is its spectacular
disarray. The music turning toward light
shadows. O god of the healing art
where is the beautiful lyre of the body?

❦

WHAT I MEAN, I GUESS, IS THIS

A boy
gathers up his shirt beneath a cloud,
the sun, and it is spring,
the light clear and hard
like the birdsong that trills all over
these darker portions of

the body. What I mean, I guess, is this.
How can a desire become perfected
yet still remain
desire? As when a boy,

unaware, finds
his mother dressing,
and sees her breasts' dark aureoles
suddenly splashed with light,

and turns his head away
except for eyes
that keep on swimming
until his mind crawls back inside
the lovely cave

of her. Sleep is
not a form
of prayer. Not
really. Outside it tries

to shower, and soon
it does with sun. The wet asphalt
shining all at once,
all the sparrows chatter.

And suddenly I want to trace
with red chalk
on faint green paper
the outline of your body.
Things take so

long. No
not really. But listen,
please. Desire everything you
want, but let the ghost
inside you linger.

❧

HEART

It snowed, a white beyond our knowing, and then
it snowed some more. The people, they were astounded
as if some thing were born

of nothing, for that whiteness made an everything
from nothing, a nothing we could not name
but to which we prayed, prayed without knowing,

which seemed the only way, now
that our century darkened, darkened to a close,
and we were less, less than something whole,

for we had murdered something we could
not name, and that something fell, fell
more beautifully in its blankness

and in its cold, a cold that blew beyond
our knowing, and beyond our hearts' desire to know.

❧❧❧

ACKNOWLEDGMENTS

The author would like to thank the editors of the following magazines and periodicals where many of these poems originally appeared: *Agni Review, The American Poetry Review, The Atlantic, Black Warrior Review, The Bloomsbury Review, Boulevard, The Denver Quarterly, The Kenyon Review, The Laurel Review, The Mid-American Review, The Paris Review, Pequod, The Nation, The New England Review, The Ohio Review, Shenandoah, Volt, Western Humanities Review.*

"Robert Mapplethorpe's Photograph of Apollo" (1988), which originally appeared in *The Paris Review*, was also reprinted in *The Pushcart Prize XIX: Best of the Small Presses.*

"Turbo-Descartes" originally appeared in *The Denver Quarterly*.

"J.F.K.'s 45th Birthday: Madison Square Garden" originally appeared in the anthology *Marilyn, My Marilyn*, Pennywhistle Press, Santa Fe, N.M.

Thanks to Jorie Graham, John Hobbs, and Bin Ramke for editorial suggestions. And to Al Poulin.

I would also like to thank the National Endowment for the Arts for an Individual Fellowship which allowed me to complete many of these poems. Special thanks to Henry Sauerwein of the Wurlitzer Foundation in Taos, N.M., to Nolan Rucker-Sauvage of Cuchara Valley Ranch, and to Reyes García of Antonito, all of whom provided me with places of spirit.

M.I.

❧

ABOUT THE AUTHOR

Mark Irwin was born in Faribault, Minnesota, in 1953, and has lived throughout the United States and abroad in France and Italy. He has taught at a number of universities, including Case Western Reserve, the University of Iowa, Ohio University, and the University of Denver. He is the author of two previous collections: *The Halo of Desire*, Galileo Press, 1987; and *Against the Meanwhile (3 Elegies)*, Wesleyan University Press, 1989. He has also translated two volumes of poetry. His awards include the "Discovery" / *The Nation* Award, a Pushcart Prize, National Endowment for the Arts and Ohio Arts Council Fellowships, and a Fulbright Fellowship to Romania. He lives with his family in Denver, Colorado.

❦

BOA EDITIONS, LTD.
AMERICAN POETS CONTINUUM SERIES

❧❧❧